Jelly is on the wall looking at all the rubbish in the dump.

She sees something move among the rubbish. Is it a rat?

Jelly goes down the plank to have a look for it.

She sees bags, bottles, pans and a lamp, but nothing moves.

Then she sees a basket by the wall. A red cloth is on the basket.

Is the rat under the cloth? Jelly pats the cloth to feel for it.

A very cross cat jumps up from the basket.
'Help', thinks Jelly.

She runs back to the wall and jumps over it as fast as she can.